21-Day

Weight Release Journey

Create the Best Version of YOU:

Mind, Body & Soul

By Jackie Harden

<u>Dedication</u>

This book is dedicated
to all the women of the world who had
the courage to wake up
and get out of bed today.
You are more powerful
than you know.
I acknowledge you!
I celebrate you!
I'm here to cheer you on!
May the Ultimate Power of the
Universe lead you to
fulfill your destiny!

"May the God of hope fill you with all
joy and peace as you trust in Him, so
that you may overflow with hope by
the power of the Holy Spirit."
~ Romans 15:13 (NIV)

"Wishing you love, peace,
and joy overflowing"
~ Jackie Harden

Table of Contents

Part 3 – The Soul

INTRODUCTION

Welcome to the 21-Day Weight Release Journey! I am so glad you are here!

Before we begin this journey, I encourage you to get a journal specifically for the purpose of writing down what comes up for you over the next 21 days. If you choose to keep your notes on your computer, that's perfectly fine. Just make sure to keep your notes together in one folder so you can easily refer back to what you've written each day. Next, get your mind right. What does that mean? Simply, set your intention. Commit to showing up for yourself consistently for 21 days. Think about what you really want for your life. What does that look like for you? Ask yourself right now, "what do I really want"? What will it cost if you do not release what is weighing on you? How will it feel to be free?

Consider what you have done for other people that you care about. And those same gifts and talents that you poured into your family, that you pour into your children, that you pour into your husband, your job, call upon that same energy, those same gifts, those same skills, and those same talents right now. This is for you!

I submit that my most important job has always been the role of mother. When I think about all that it took for me to raise my daughter, to pour into my daughter, to want more for my daughter, to be a good mother for my daughter, I know that all those gifts and talents that I called upon to push myself to create a better life for her are still within me. I remember calling on a power greater than myself and asking God to look past my faults to see my need to be a good mother for my daughter. I remember working two and three jobs, going to school to get my college degree, showing up no matter what, getting past my own fears, my own insecurities, because I wanted more for my daughter. At that time, my focus was on creating a better life for her, but the by-product of my effort resulted in a better life for us (myself included). The moral of the story is that when we help other people, whether it is a family member, a friend, or a total stranger, the reciprocal law of the universe ensures that we also reap the benefits.

So right now, I want you to declare what it is that you want to accomplish over the next 21 days. Get your mind right, set your intention and declare right now what it is that you want. Dream big, stretch yourself, go for it ALL. Write it down.

Of all the things you want for your life, what do you want to focus on right now? What is that one thing that over the next 21 days you are going to focus on? It may require sacrifice. It will require discipline and it will require focused intention. We are going to walk this out together, one day at a time. So, what is it: Improved health? Increased happiness and joy? More energy? A better career? Improved relationships? Better relationships? What is it? Declare it! Let's make it happen. I want you to win.

When you think about losing something, and you alternatively think about releasing it, what goes through your mind? According to Webster's dictionary, when you lose something, you become unable to find it. When you lose something, it is considered a loss. However, when you release something, you set it free. It's your decision to let it go. Whatever the "it" is for you. Releasing "it" puts you in a position of power.

In what area of your life would you like to experience freedom? This journey is about releasing those things that hold you back so you can set yourself free to experience more of what you want in your life. While we could, no doubt, talk about releasing physical weight, there may be some other stuff weighing you down that you want to release in order to create space for more love, peace, and joy in your life.

The goal of this 21-Day Journey is to bring your Mind, Body and Soul into alignment to manifest your desired outcome. To that end, visualize what you want and imagine yourself free from whatever no longer serves your greater good and then imagine being totally filled with all the things that make your heart sing.

Let me share a little about myself. Many of you may know, that I am a single mother, a professional strategic life coach, a motivational speaker, a human resources manager with 20 years' experience, an entrepreneur and owner of Life of Victory Enterprises, LLC. You may also know that I have helped women overcome the pain of their past to create the life of their dreams. I am also a surrogate mother and grandmother, who went from bankruptcy and eviction and worked my way to become a homeowner and a successful business owner.

After working my whole life to climb out of poverty and to raise my daughter, who happens to be an extraordinarily successful businesswoman and entrepreneur in her own right, I lost my HR job. Last year was a challenging year for a lot of people. Some of us lost loved ones, some lost jobs, some lost homes, and others lost their businesses. During the challenges that the pandemic of 2020 presented, many of us even lost hope.

So, in September of 2020, I decided to create a 21-day weight release challenge and connected with people via Facebook Live with the intention to inspire and share hope. During the Facebook Live sessions, we talked about creating the best version of ourselves: Mind, Body and Soul. Many of the participants in the 21 Day Challenge wanted to focus on losing weight, physical weight that is. However, what occurred to me is that in order to actually lose the physical pounds, you need to figure out why you put on the additional pounds in the first place. Typically, women use food for comfort to avoid or to make up for something that's missing in their life. Does that sound familiar? The physical weight is a manifestation of other "weight" that is weighing you down. Have you ever wondered why gaining weight seems so easy but losing weight seems so hard?

Well, the purpose of this book is to help you look at what could be holding you back, blocking you, and keeping you stuck. No matter what is going on around you, what is going on within you is much more important. The extra pounds could be the result of other weight you are carrying but are unaware. We tend to use food for comfort to sooth the source of our discomfort, loneliness, displeasure, doubt, etc. and end up putting on extra pounds which can add to our feelings of frustration. Does that make sense? Can you relate?

Trust me I've been there too. There is no judgement here. I've just shown up to help you take a look at your pattern of behavior. And, if you're ready (and I think you are, that's why you're here) you will discover what's true for you.

Here are some examples of things that can weigh you down:

Addiction(s)	Depression	Procrastination
Anger	Doubt	Resentment
Anxiety	Fear	Sadness
Blame	Frustration	Struggle
Chaos	Grudges	Toxic People
Clutter	Health Issues	Trauma
Conflict	Lies	Uncertainty
Confusion	Loneliness	Unforgiveness
Dead Weight	Negativity	Unfulfilled Desires
Debt	Painful Memories	Worry

I am grateful that you are here. Thank you for showing up! Thank you! Thank you! Thank you! Now get ready to play full-out. Commit to reading one chapter each day and complete the journal exercises. Be honest with yourself. Write down what comes up for you and if you feel so inclined, invite someone to share this journey with you. For best results, join the free Facebook Group "Best Life Creators" to connect with others who are on this journey as well. Having a supportive community will help you stay on track and can also make this journey a lot of fun. Enjoy the process.

One of my favourite quotes is: "We don't get the life we deserve; we get the life we create." It is up to you to create the life that you want.

PART 1

THE MIND

Day 1: The Power of Your Mind

"Whatsoever things are true, whatsoever things are honest, whatsoever things are just, whatsoever things are pure, whatsoever things are lovely, whatsoever things are of good report, if there be any virtue, and if there be any praise, think on these things." ~ Philippians 4:8

It has been said that what we think about, we bring about. Another way of saying that is what our mind conceives, and we believe, we will achieve. The mind is extremely powerful, and we must consciously feed it positive information in order to reap a positive result. **"Mind power is one of the strongest and most useful powers you possess. This power, together with your**

16

imagination, can create success or failure, happiness or unhappiness, opportunities or obstacles." ~ Joseph Murphy

Your thoughts become things. Therefore, it is important to train your brain to focus on things that are good, things that are beautiful, and things that are positive. So often when things are not going the way that we want them to, we blame ourselves and engage in negative self-talk. Instead of doing that, focus your attention on the lesson learned from the experience. See the beauty that surrounds you. Focus your attention on all the things that you can be grateful for.

Keep in mind, before you release anything, create something, or achieve a goal, you must first have the thought. Even if you don't believe it's possible to achieve it right now, you must first begin to contemplate or think about the possibility. Think about what it will take to create the result you want. For instance, if you want to improve a relationship with someone, ask yourself "who do I need to be in order to improve the quality of my relationship?" Start by focusing on the relationship you have with yourself. The love you have for yourself will naturally affect every other relationship. When you feel good about yourself, that energy is contagious. What needs to happen in order for you to feel better about yourself?

Journal Activity #1: Think about your positive attributes. What have you accomplished in the past? Think about a time when you felt good. What was going on around you? How did you feel inside? What happened that contributed to your state of happiness, well-being, and joy? What do you want

more of in your life right now? What will it take to make it happen? What are the steps to get there? Write it out, step by step. Here's an affirmation for today: "I am worthy of my goals, dreams, and desires."

Whatever you want to achieve over the next 21 days, tell yourself every morning and every night before you go to sleep "I am worthy of ...." Fill in the blank with the thing you intend to be, do, or have.

Day 2: Subconscious Mind vs. Conscious Mind

"Your mind is alert; your memory is keen for you have the all-knowing mind of infinite intelligence within you." ~ Anonymous

Your mind will believe and act upon whatever you tell it. Therefore, it is important to pay attention to your thoughts, especially the thoughts you have about yourself. Your thoughts create emotions. Emotions create action. And your actions create results.

Your thoughts can trigger positive or negative emotions. If you tell yourself that you're not worthy of success, your mind will believe it and act upon the information you've given it. However, when you tell yourself that you are worthy of financial wealth and abundance, your mind will believe that as well and will go into action to make that statement come true. You will be supercharged to figure out how to tap into the frequency of abundance and prosperity.

Your subconscious mind is always working. It is most fertile first thing in the morning as you are breaking sleep and late at night when you are about to go to sleep. Particularly at these times what you tell yourself will set the tone for the day and determine what settles in at night. Try starting each day thanking God for your life, health, and strength. Set your intention for a good day and thank God for the great news you will receive today. Additionally, prior to going to sleep, show gratitude for all the wonderful blessings of the day. Tell yourself that you are strong, healthy, happy, whole, and financially abundant. Your mind will believe what you tell it, and your subconscious mind will internalize it.

When you decide to release negative thoughts and begin replacing them with positive thoughts, your entire outlook will change because you are feeding your mind with uplifting thoughts. The more you put this into practice the greater your results. As soon as a negative thought enters your mind, it is your responsibility to flood your mind with positive thoughts to prevent the negative thought from taking hold.

Journal Activity #2: Write down three gratitude statements you will tell yourself today. Start first thing in the morning. And create three powerful statements that you want for your life.

For example, I am happy, healthy, and financially abundant. I release all struggle and anxiety for I know God is with me always. I release my fear of lack and accept the abundance and prosperity of the universe.

Day 3: The Power of Focused Intention

**"Intention is a force in the universe, and everything and everyone is connected to this invisible force."
~ Dr. Wayne W. Dyer**

What you focus on expands. Many think that there is no need to affirm and repeat a mantra, but I have learned otherwise. The reason we journal, repeat mantras and recite positive affirmations is to help the mind focus on the intended result. These practices of repetition help us change our mindset. As you get in the habit of focusing on what you want, you will begin to see greater possibilities. Your desires will manifest and expand into your reality.

Energy flows where focus goes. Give yourself permission to dream big. Focus on the most excellent possibility for your life. If things are not going the way you want, maybe you need to change your focus. Focus so hard that you see nothing else but what you want, what you desire, and what you deserve. Focus on the end goal, and the end goal will keep you going. Visualize it and pursue it with all you've got.

Journal Activity #3: Write five gratitude statements and set your intentions for your day and night's sleep. What will you focus on? Choose an area of your life and write down what you are willing to create. What is your primary focus for your life right now? What is your utmost desire?

Day 4: Think Big

**"As a man thinketh in his heart,
so is he." ~ Proverbs 23:7**

You have probably heard it said many times that what you focus on EXPANDS. Have you ever purchased a new car? And, as soon as you get the car, you notice all the cars that look just like yours. Why is that? Because now that you have the new car, you're focusing your attention on all the cars that look like yours. They were always there you just did not notice them until you focused your attention on them.

That is true for everything in your life. What you focus on will expand! What you think about, you bring about! Your focused attention on the thing you want will set your thoughts in action to manifest it.

Thoughts become things. That is another reason why it is important to stay in gratitude. As you focus your attention on your blessings, you will receive more blessings. As you think about all the beauty around you, you will create more beauty. As you think about all the money you have received up to this point in your life and show gratitude for it, you will receive more money. I could go on and on about the benefits of gratitude and focused intention, but I want you to think about this principle and how it is true for you.

When you focus on lack, you will experience more lack. If you have a scarcity mindset, you will continue to experience limited resources. Conversely, when you focus your attention on your goal and create a plan of action steps to get there, it's inevitable that you will achieve your goal. There is nothing like a made-up mind. Once you decide to go for your goal and take deliberate, consistent action towards the achievement of your goal, you are destined to achieve it.

So, THINK BIG! DREAM BIG! And stay in action. Even if you only take small steps forward, you're still moving in the right direction. If you'll just keep moving forward, eventually you will get there. The journey of a thousand miles starts by taking the first step.

Journal Activity #4: Write five gratitude statements and set your intentions for your day and night's sleep. What will you focus on? Choose an area of your life and write down what you are willing to create. What is your primary focus for your life right now? What is your utmost desire? THINK BIG!

Day 5: Miracle Working Power

"Do not be anxious about anything, but in every situation, by prayer and petition, with thanksgiving, present your requests to God. And the peace of God, which transcends all understanding, will guard your hearts and your minds in Christ Jesus." ~ Philippians 1:6-7

When was the last time that you focused on your breathing? When was the last time you deliberately stopped what you were doing to take a deep breath?

Yes, we breathe every second, but we don't always set time aside to breathe deeply, meditate, and pray. We tend to take in short breaths as we go about our daily routine. Try making it a habit to breathe deeply a few times every day.

As you breathe-in, imagine that you are inhaling positive energy. As you exhale, imagine that you are releasing toxic negative energy. Repeat this exercise a few times and notice your body's response. Each time you inhale and exhale, allow yourself to experience the flow of energy through your body.

Here's a short list of the benefits of deep breathing:

- Decreases stress.
- Reduces tension and heightens your sense of calm.
- Relieves pain and stimulates the lymphatic system which purifies the body.
- Improves immunity and increases energy.

Prayer and Meditation

Many people think that prayer and meditation are only for religious people. That couldn't be farther from the truth. The truth is that when you invoke the power of the Ultimate Force of the Universe, you set a powerful force into action on your behalf. I don't purport to have all the answers, but one thing I do know is that prayer works. I have come to know that when you turn your situation, your goals, your desires, over to a power greater than yourself and believe that it's possible for an all-knowing, omnipotent God to work on your behalf, it's sure to come to fruition. You've also got to do your part and stay in action. *"Faith without works is dead"* James 2:26. But I'm a living witness that through prayer and meditation, God will do more than you can think, ask, or imagine.

Journal Activity #5: Consider the following questions and write about what comes up for you: What are you holding on to that no longer serves a positive purpose in your life? When you release it, what will you create in its place? When it comes to holding on to something or someone that doesn't serve your greater good, just know that it is taking up space for something else (something better). It is acting as a distraction or is blocking you from experiencing something greater.

Show yourself grace and thank "Ultimate Intelligence" for bringing you to an awareness that it's time to release the distraction, the negativity, and anything that is blocking you from getting what you want. If it no longer serves your greater good, let it go.

Make deep breathing, prayer and meditation a part of your daily routine and notice how you feel. Then write about it in your journal.

Day 6: Powerful Conversations

**"What other people think of me is
none of my business."
~ Eleanor Roosevelt**

The most powerful conversation you will have today is the conversation with yourself. What you think about yourself will determine what you say to yourself. What is the message you typically send to yourself about yourself? Is it a message of love and acceptance? Is it a message of encouragement and admiration? Or is it a message of doubt and degradation?

Whatever you think will affect how you feel, and your feelings affect your behavior. With that being the case, how important do you think it is to upgrade your thoughts about yourself? Pretty important, right?!

You might ask: how do I upgrade my thoughts about myself? By using positive affirmations, you can improve how you feel about yourself, thereby improving your behavior.

I used to struggle with feelings of unworthiness. I used to lament about my past and without realizing it, I was holding myself hostage to the old version of myself and wasn't giving myself permission to step into a new and improved version of myself. Through coaching, I became aware that I was beating myself up with negative self-talk. I had to train my brain to think powerful thoughts about myself. So, anytime a negative thought would come up, I flooded my mind with positive affirmations.

Here are some of the affirmations I use daily. Try using these affirmations or create some of your own.

I am Happy.
I am Healthy, Wealthy, and Wise.
I am Secure.
I am Worthy.
I am Positive.
I am Beautiful, Loved, and Blessed.
I am Grateful.
I am Confident.
I am Courageous.
I am Excited About Today.

Journal Activity #6: Create positive affirmations for yourself or use the ones provided above. Write them on post-it notes, and post them on the bathroom mirror, near your computer at work, or on the dashboard of your car. Post them anywhere you are sure to notice them, so you are reminded of your greatness. Say them in the morning and all throughout the day. Continue to write at least five gratitude statements every day.

Day 7: Declare Your Victory

"Whatever you declare for your life and take action to manifest will happen." ~ Jackie Harden

Right here right now declare your victory! Declare victory over limitation, loss, and doubt. Declare yourself a winner, an achiever, an overcomer, and a conqueror. You have the power within to accomplish any goal you set for yourself. See yourself having what you want. Set the vision in your mind's eye and see it done. See it accomplished. See it achieved. You have already begun to THINK BIG and if you've gotten to Day 7 of the 21-Day Journey to Create the Best Version of You: Mind, Body and Soul that means that you're staying in action. I celebrate you for staying the course. Keep up the good work!

How has the first week of this journey been for you? Are you seeing results? Are you staying in action? Do you need to make adjustments to get on track to achieve your goal? What is your plan of action? Are you implementing it? Are there any obstacles standing in your way? What steps are you willing to take to remove all distractions, obstacles, and excuses. What do you need help with? Who can you ask to support you? Focus on the goal. Declare your victory!

Journal Activity #7: Write the answers to the questions above. Write about how you will feel when you achieve your goal. Be descriptive. Celebrate your progress. Notice what you are thinking, feeling, and experiencing. Stay in gratitude!

Part 2

THE BODY

Day 8: Your Body is a Temple

"Know ye not that your body is the temple of the Holy Ghost, which is in you..." ~ 1 Corinthians 6:19

Your body is an amazing system that supports you every day. You only get one and it has to last your entire lifetime. With that in mind, it is wise to care for your body to the best of our ability. Every part of the body has a purpose and a specific job to do. There are 12 systems of the body. These body systems include the skeletal, nervous, muscular, respiratory, endocrine, immune, cardiovascular/ circulatory, urinary, integumentary, reproductive, and digestive systems. It stands to reason that if one system

41

malfunctions, it creates dis-ease and can adversely impact your state of well-being.

Consider how many times your heart beats in one day, and how it never stops beating. Your heart is always working for you. It beats consistently without you having to ask or question it. Have you ever stopped to thank your heart for beating? Do you take it for granted that your heart will beat all day every day? What do you do to ensure the health of your heart? How about the other vital organs in your body? Have you thought about what is required for your body to function at optimal level? If not, today take some time to think about the miraculous bodily system you have.

If your body is not performing at optimal level, what are you willing to do to make improvements? Will you decrease the amount of sugar and salt you ingest? Will you eat more vegetables and fewer fried foods? Will you begin to incorporate exercise into your daily routine? Will you drink more water and fewer carbonated beverages?

Your body is a gift from God. What you do with it is your gift to God.

Journal Activity #8: Write five gratitude statements for and about your body. Then decide what action you will take to improve your health and well-being.

Day 9: You Are in Control of Your Physical Body

"A healthy mindset is a key component to a healthy body." ~ Inc.com

By changing the way you think and becoming more aware of what occupies your mind, you can vastly improve your physical health and well-being. When you focus on what is missing in your life and you allow yourself to worry about situations and circumstances that are beyond your control, it increases the likelihood of depression or stress. However, when you focus on all that you do have and show gratitude, you are more likely to experience joy.

As previously stated, what you think about elicits feelings within your body and it is your feelings that fuel your actions. If you are constantly stressed out, worried, anxious, and/or angry, eventually it will make you sick. Have you noticed that when you get upset, you typically end up with a headache, a stomach-ache, or a backache? The mental anguish manifests itself in your body. And oftentimes we dismiss or neglect what our body is telling us until it becomes a major problem, such as a heart attack, a stroke, or cancer.

Listen to your body but more importantly I want you to realize that you are in control of your physical body. It may not be easy to think positive when something bad happens. But if you practice finding beauty in all things and focus on what you can be grateful for, I promise you that you will begin to feel better. Your positive outlook will help you to find a way through whatever life circumstance you find yourself in. You absolutely have the power within you to create the emotional state you desire.

The tragedies of life can weigh you down if you allow them to. Believe me, I completely understand that some things are easier to get over than others. But no matter what happens in life, you get to choose your response. Unforeseen occurrences befall us all. As you proceed forward to the achievement of your goal, stay in faith, practice positive thinking, and listen to what your body is telling you.

Journal Activity #9: Continue stating affirmations to uplift your spirit. What actions will you take today to care for yourself? Be kind to yourself and do something nice for yourself (i.e., soak in the tub, dance, go for a walk). Then write about how caring for yourself made you feel.

Day 10: Your Body's Response to Weight

**"A heart at peace gives life to the body, but envy rots the bones."
~ Proverbs 14:30**

What weight are you carrying that you'd like to release? Is it self-doubt, anger, procrastination? What is the weight costing you? What has to happen for you to let go and make a change?

We are on Day 10 of the Weight Release Journey and it's time to check-in with yourself to assess where you are. What progress have you made? What haven't you done that you wanted to accomplish? What has distracted you? From where you are right now, what are you committed to do from this point forward to move you closer to your goal?

I encourage you to show yourself some grace. There's no need to beat-up on yourself or compare yourself to somebody else. When you compare yourself to somebody else you waste energy and deprive yourself of seeing your own value. There is always somebody better, faster, or smarter. But that doesn't need to steal your joy. Celebrate who you are and what you bring to the table. You are enough. You are beautiful loved and blessed. And you matter.

Journal Activity #10: Here are questions to help you release the weight. In your journal, write the answers to the following questions and notice what comes up for you.

Is there anything you would do differently if you had the chance? It is said that we are as sick as our secrets. What secrets are you keeping? What does it cost you to keep those secrets? How honest are you willing to be with yourself and others to achieve the peace of mind you deserve?

Re-commit, re-focus, and re-calibrate. You get to decide what you are willing to do to release the weight. In the meantime, love yourself, forgive yourself, and stay in gratitude.

Day 11: The Choice is Yours

"The ultimate measure of a man is not where he stands in moments of comfort and convenience, but where he stands in times of challenge and controversy." ~ Martin L. King, Jr.

Where you are in life is the result of the choices and decisions you've made. Many times, we don't want to take responsibility for the choices we've made because it's easier to blame someone else. However, when we get honest with ourselves and take a good hard look at what's driving us to do the things we do, the way we do it, we might discover that we have the power to make a change. We can decide to choose differently. Just because you've been arriving late to work every day doesn't mean that you can't make a decision to get up earlier so that you can do what you need to do in the morning and have enough time to arrive to work on or before your scheduled start time.

In terms of your diet, just because you've gained 30 pounds during the COVID-19 pandemic, doesn't mean that you have to continue to eat the foods that resulted in weight gain. You can choose to make better food choices that will result in weight release.

The choice is yours. So, what are you choosing? Moving forward, what will you choose? Will you choose love? Will you choose peace? Will you choose joy? Will you choose YOU? What will that look like?

Many people get stuck in the challenges of life. Unanticipated things can and do happen. But what happens to you isn't nearly as important as what happens within you. Life is 10 percent what happens to you and 90 percent how you respond. Two people can have the same experience but respond totally different. How you choose to respond will determine your emotional state and the actions you will or will not take.

It's been said that if we focus on our problems, then our God is small. Focus on how big God is. With faith in a power greater than yourself nothing is impossible. It may take time to overcome tragedy, trauma, or loss but in time things will get better. Do not allow yourself to become bitter. Instead, choose to become better. One day at a time watch your circumstances improve.

Do your best and God will do the rest. However, it doesn't start with doing; it starts with being. Do you want love? Then be loving.

Do you want peace? Then be peaceful and bring peace to the situation.

The choice is yours to be, do, and have. Ask yourself, who do I need to be, what do I need to do to have what I want. Release the weight to become the best version of you.

Journal Activity #11: Today, take time to write a Love Letter to yourself. Show yourself love for who you are and what you've accomplished thus far in life. Who will you commit to being and what will you commit to doing, to have the life you know you deserve? The choice is yours to release the weight and take action to create the best version of yourself one day at a time.

Reminder: If you always do, what you've always done. You'll always get what you've always gotten.

Day 12: Be Bold About Getting Unblocked

"Be bold and mighty forces will come to your aid." ~ Basil King

Is there anything standing in the way of you creating the life you want? How would life be different for you if you had the life of your dreams? Have you ever taken time to visualize the life that you "really" want and then write it down?

Too often we make excuses about not doing the things we said we would do to save money to buy a new house, to lose weight, to obtain that degree, to start our own business, to learn a new language. Sometimes what's standing in the way is our limiting beliefs, such as I'm not good enough, I'm not smart enough, I'm not worthy of it, etc. etc. etc.

What are you telling yourself about your BIG DREAM? You see, most of us have to come to the realization that we have to get out of our own way. Get rid of negative self-talk and go for the goal. If you have a dream, a goal, or a desire to achieve something BIG, the thought never would have come into your mind if you weren't fully capable of bringing it to fruition. Yes, you may have to study, work, and sacrifice. But if you really want to achieve the goal then you need to accept what it will take to get there.

Research people who have already done what you're trying to do. Find out what course of action they took and model that. Get involved with a support group of like-minded people. Find your tribe! Everything becomes easier when you have support.

Sometimes we are afraid of our own beauty, success, and sexiness. We are afraid of getting that thing we really want. We wonder about the attention success will bring, or we convince ourselves that we don't deserve it. So, we sabotage ourselves and remain comfortable in that place of mediocrity. Visualize yourself at your best and boldly work towards the next chapter of your life.

Journal Activity #12: Take a look at where you are now and where you would like to be. If you knew you couldn't fail, what would you do differently? How would life be for you if you released the weight you've been holding onto? What do you want to change in your life, and how would life be if you made those changes? What's the vision for your life? What does it look like? What does it feel like? Can you visualize the life you want to create? After writing the answers to the questions above in your journal, create a vision board. Put everything you want and know you deserve on the board.

Day 13: Press Forward – No Matter What!

"This one thing I do, forgetting those things which are behind, and reaching forth unto those things which are before, I press toward the mark for the prize of the high calling of God" ~ Philippians 3:13-14

Back in the day, before the advent of CDs and DVDs, we had cassette tapes. We used cassette tapes when we wanted to record something from the radio or any other medium. We used blank tapes for every recording. However, if we didn't have a blank tape, we would use a cassette tape that had content on it and record over it to override what was on there.

At the beginning of this 21-Day Journey, we talked about the power of the mind and how we can change how we feel simply by changing what we think about. What you focus your attention on is what will manifest. When you change the conversation you have internally, from negative, self-defeating language to more positive empowering language, you create a more positive outlook, thereby manifesting positive behavior.

No matter what you want in your life, it is up to you to get there. What are you thinking about? What are you focusing your attention on? What consistent actions are you taking to achieve your goal? You are fully equipped to do whatever God has purposed for your life. Transform your thoughts; transform your life. That is the truth!

The lie is that it is impossible. The lie is that you can't achieve your goal. Don't fall for the lie. It is up to you to choose success because success is already within you. Make the decision to press forward and don't you dare give up. There is no guarantee that you'll succeed the first time you try, but if you don't try at all, it's certain that you won't succeed. So, try, try, and try again... until you win. As Les Brown has said: "It's not over until YOU win!"

Do not look back at your failures. If you fail, fail forward and learn the lesson your mistake showed up to teach you. Failure is feedback. If you fail, get the lesson. If you don't apply the lessons learned, you'll keep going around in circles, failing and getting feedback until you break the cycle.

Remember: failure is not fatal, and success is not final. There is always another level. No matter what has happened in your past you get to create a bright future.

Journal Activity #13: Show gratitude for the battles you have faced, fought, and overcome, which brought you to where you are now. Declare for yourself that you will not give up on your dreams, goals, and desires. What action will you take today to move closer to your goal?

"Never let success get to your head; never let failure get to your heart."
~ Anonymous

Day 14: Stay in Action

"We are what we repeatedly do. Excellence, then, is not an act but a habit." ~ Aristotle

We tend to focus our attention on those around us; our family, friends, and co-workers but neglect to stay in action towards the achievement of our own goals, dreams, and desires. Sometimes we need to take a leap of faith and ask for help. The help, support, and assistance may require a financial investment; whatever is required is available. The question is: Are you willing to invest in yourself to get the information and support that you need?

Investing in yourself means staying in action for yourself, for your business, and ultimately for your goals, dreams, and desires to come to fruition. Are you willing to invest the time, money, and effort to learn how to develop a business mindset? To develop a wealth mindset. To learn to speak another language. You get the idea. Investing in yourself could simply mean setting time aside to do something you enjoy or something new that you've talked about doing but haven't yet done. Nothing will change unless you make a move. Consistent intentional action is the key to results.

You may be wondering: What do I do when I don't know what I don't know? Or, you may know that you don't know but you don't know who can help you get the information, skills, and training that you need. I encourage you to research your field of interest to find out what resources are available. There is a plethora of information on the internet that can point you in the right direction.

Invest in a personal trainer, a coach, or a mentor to help you get closer to where you want to be. In sports, the most amazing athletes hire a coach to sharpen their skills. You can't see your own ears. So, having a person in your corner to help you see your blind spots can make all the difference in the world. Work with someone who has done what you're trying to do and is willing to support and guide you along your path to success.

Your success isn't only about you, anyway. There is someone waiting for you. There is someone out there who needs what you have to offer. There is someone praying right now for you to show up in their life. Will you answer the call and become the answer to the prayer? Become all that you can be and bless others as you build. Invest in yourself and live the life to which you are called.

Journal Activity #14: Stay in action. Consistent Small Wins Create Big Wins! Write about the action you have taken thus far on this journey and the results you've gotten. If you haven't taken action, notice what you've been telling yourself and take action to change the conversation to one that is empowering, uplifting, and will motivate you to action. Research your field of interest to find out what resources are available.

Part 3

THE SOUL

Day 15: "Stretch Out on Faith and Let the Miracle Happen" ~ Jackie Harden

Tune in to Spirit and notice the wonder-working powers all around you. Your soul knows what you need and want right now. So, why not stretch out on faith and let the miracle appear. Miracles happen every day. You deserve your miracle. Trust and believe, God's got a miracle with your name on it. Stretch out on faith and let the miracle happen for you.

What is faith? From a biblical perspective, Hebrews 11:1 says, "Now faith is the substance of things hoped for, and the evidence of things not seen." It takes faith to believe that the impossible (what you cannot see) is possible (what you can see). "Truly I tell you, if you have faith as small as a mustard seed, you can say to the mountain, 'move from here to there,' and it will move." Matthew 17:20

What is that mountain that you want to move?

Everyone is either recovering from an experience with a mountain, presently in an experience with a mountain, or about to get into an experience with a mountain. We all get to face a mountain at one time or another in our life. Right now, your mountain is that weight you want to release. That thing you want to free yourself from, the confusion around how to create the business you want to create. In order to move the mountain, you must first believe. Believe in yourself and a power greater than yourself. Trust Ultimate Intelligence, Ultimate Wisdom, the God of your understanding to move your mountain.

One way to stretch out on faith is to create space for the thing you want to manifest. You won't get the blessed relationship you want by holding on to the toxic relationship you're in. Letting go can be scary even when it's something you know is holding you back, keeping you stuck, and causing you pain (i.e., debt, doubt, divorce, negativity, clutter, confusion, anger, resentment, and physical weight). When we get comfortable carrying the weight of the mountain, it becomes normal. It becomes our comfort zone.

Let me tell you a story about my mountain. I had to come to grips with the fact that I've been pre-disposed to dysfunction. In terms of my personal relationship, I tolerated behavior that was totally out of control far longer than I should have. Even though I knew I had to end the toxic relationship, I was afraid of the repercussions of ending it. As a result, I went above and beyond to help my significant other at the time to get his life together so he could move out of my house peacefully. Long story short, even after buying him a new car, helping him get a full-time job with benefits, and an apartment, he broke into my house, stole my money, stalked me, called my employer to say only God knows what about me. Obviously, he wanted to destroy me. Had I just kicked him to the curb, I would have saved myself a lot of time, heart ache, and money.

We tend to think that the mountain will never move. However, when you decide to make it move, change is certain. As it turned out, my Ex- ended up in jail. He continued to stalk and harass me and was finally arrested. It was clear that I wanted to help him land on his feet when he left my house. But it became clear to me that he took my kindness for weakness and wanted to take all that I had created: my money, my house, and my life. He was determined to destroy me. But I refused to let him intimidate me. I refused to succumb to his angry tirades and threats of violence.

Have you ever allowed yourself to get stuck in the fear of the unknown? Are you caught up in the what ifs? What if it doesn't work out? What if I don't have enough money to make it on my own? Fear is the opposite of faith, and if you want to fly, release your fear and trust that everything will work out. It always does! It takes courage to activate faith. But, when you surrender to the Ultimate Power of the Universe and believe in the power, wisdom, and strength of the Almighty, miracles happen.

You do not get the life you deserve; you get the life you create. It's up to you to align your Mind, Body and Soul with the Ultimate Power Source around and within you to create the life you envision. Keep the faith! Stretch out on Faith and Let the Miracle Happen!

Journal Activity #15: Write about one thing you keep putting off. What's holding you back? What do you fear? What has the fear, doubt, and procrastination cost you? And, what has to happen for you to stretch out on faith to remove that mountain?

"Now faith is the substance of things hoped for and the evidence of things not seen."
~ Hebrews 11:1

Day 16: What Do You Believe?

"Belief comes before the victory."
~ Anonymous

The most important ingredient in the recipe of success is belief in yourself and your ability. Whatever you think is possible for your life is what you will create. All things are possible if you believe. If you can imagine more for your life and create a clear vision for it, you can achieve it. Consider every area of your life: your relationships, your finances, your career, your health, and your spirituality. Are you where you want to be in every area of your life? Most people strive to improve in at least one area of their life.

Think about your beliefs. Do you believe you are worthy of healthy relationships? Do you believe you deserve financial freedom? Do you believe it's possible to have the career of your dreams? Do you believe you can create your own business? Do you believe health and wellness can be yours? What about spirituality? Do you have a spiritual life? What do you believe?

Whatever you believe will drive your behavior. If you believe you are worthy of the best, that is what you expect. You won't settle for mediocrity. **Belief – 1. an acceptance that a statement is true or that something exists. 2. trust, faith, or confidence in someone or something. Fact – a thing that is known or proved to be true.**

What happens around you isn't nearly as important as what happens within you. Things won't always work out the way you want them to, but your attitude will always determine your disposition. Maintaining a positive "can do" attitude will help you figure your way up, out, or through. As you proceed toward the achievement of your goal, I encourage you to elevate your belief in your ability.

Stay in gratitude for all that you have. Stay in action for all that you want to have. Stay in faith about the person you are and your ability to be, do, and have whatever you set your mind on. This is your time, right now, and I hope you can feel me cheering you on to VICTORY!

Journal Activity #16: Write about your experience on this 21-Day Journey. Are you making progress? What is your mindset? Are you staying in gratitude? Are you staying in action? Have you committed yourself to repeat powerful affirmations daily? What do you believe about yourself and your ability to achieve your goal?

Day 17: Search Your Soul

"Your role is to do you so well that you SHIFT your own history and come into the mystery of an unfolding soul that is always just getting started." ~ Michael Beckwith

Your soul knows the truth. Deep down in your heart and soul you know that you deserve to release whatever has been holding you back. I'm not talking about unrealistic goals but those things that are attainable, like releasing negative emotions, toxic relationships, debt, doubt, or dead weight. I'm talking about clearing the clutter, chaos, and confusion from your life.

If you're not in action to get to where you want to be, your soul will continue to be uneasy until you take action. Your soul knows if you're doing everything you need to do to release the weight. You can't hide from yourself. You can't fool yourself. It's easy to blame other people for your unhappiness but the truth is that you're responsible for your own happiness in every aspect of your life.

Your life is constantly unfolding. As you achieve one goal, you'll want to set a new one. As human beings, we have an innate desire to learn and grow. If you aren't growing, then you're dying. At a cellular level, you know what drives you and what feeds your soul. When you hold on to the people or things that are not in alignment with your true nature (your soul), it creates internal conflict. This internal conflict, if not resolved, will result in discomfort, dis-ease, or some kind of difficulty.

From my own personal experience, I have learned the value of letting go of negative thoughts, toxic people, and limiting beliefs. There was a time when I thought I would never complete my undergraduate degree course work. I thought I would never be able to purchase a home. I even thought that I would never have a loving authentic romantic relationship. I had adopted the limiting belief that I was not good enough. I wasn't worthy. I didn't matter; my feelings didn't matter; I wasn't important. If you read my memoir, "When a Lie Becomes the Truth," you know that I had to face and overcome lies, loss, and deception.

When I gave birth to my daughter, I knew that I wanted a better life for her, but I had no idea how things would work out. Even though I've made major mistakes along the way, my soul knew my true intentions. Through prayer, supplication, and consistent action, my life changed dramatically. I went from abused and addicted to create a life of abundance. I went from bankruptcy to having a six-figure income. I went from living in a studio apartment to purchasing two homes. I went from not having a college degree to obtaining two college degrees after my daughter was nearly grown. The moral of the story: search your soul and never give up on your dreams.

I've had to release a lot of bad habits and toxic people. But I'm here to tell you that your tests can become your testimony. Stay focused. Stay in faith. And take action in the direction of your goal.

Journal Activity #17: Take inventory of your life. What have you already overcome? What goals have you already achieved? What have you learned from your past experiences? Challenging experiences help to develop character and resilience. What have you learned about yourself? How can this information serve you right now and prepare you for the life you're creating?

Day 18: Surrender to Spirit

"I am the way, the truth and the life: no [wo]man cometh unto the Father but by me." ~ John 14:6

Your soul already knows what you need to release to get the result you want. The Ultimate Power of the Universe, Infinite Intelligence, Spirit (the God of your understanding) is waiting to reveal Himself to you. The moment you let go and surrender, you will see things get better. It may be subtle or sudden, but things will get better. When you've done all you can do in your own power to release the weight, it's time to turn it over.

Spirit is omnipotent, everywhere, and always available. Spirit is available to carry you and to give you peace. So, get out of your own way and surrender in prayer and meditation. Give yourself permission to feel. Feelings are not facts and whatever is showing up in your life can provide an awareness to the lesson and can become the blessing you've been asking for. There is always an opportunity to surrender to the Higher Power and draw closer to the almighty, powerful Presence that will lead and guide you. Get out of your own way.

Surrender to Spirit. Turn your battles, your struggles, your insecurities, and your doubts over. Let go. Surrender. Allow yourself to be set free. Trust and let yourself fly. The Ultimate Power of the Universe will deliver you so well and so completely that when you tell your story, it will sound unbelievable. People will find it hard to believe that you went through all the stuff you survived because you look so good, polished, and poised. It's called Divine Intervention.

Journal Activity #18: What can you experience if/when you decide to let go and turn your struggle over to Spirit. What will you have space for when you release the weight? Surrender to the Spirit and soar.

Day 19: Tell the Truth

"The voice of truth speaks to us every single day and it is as loud as our willingness to listen. Your dark chapter is not the whole book." ~ Mary Morrissey

Truth has a wonderful way of setting you free. Truth leaves nothing to hide, nothing to manipulate or intoxicate. Truth is what it is, beautiful, messy, and all that's in between. During this 21-Day Journey, you've had an opportunity to look at your life's journey. By now, I'm sure you realize that you're a work in progress. Everyone is a work in progress.

Your story is still being written by the actions you take right now. The story of your past can provide valuable information about who you are, your patterns of behavior, your strengths, your weaknesses, etc.

Accepting ALL of who you are is an important step forward to becoming ALL of who you want to be. This requires taking a hard, honest, look at yourself. What is your truth?

Most people don't want to share all their mistakes, missteps, and mishaps. I get it. Sometimes the fear of being judged can hold you hostage. And it's not the judgement of others that is most crippling; it's your self-judgement. It's the inner critic that tells you you're not enough, you're stupid, you're ugly, you're unlovable, and so on, and so on. When you get to a place where you can stand on your story, realizing that you are the sum-total of all your experiences, you are on your way to self-love. Change your story. Change your life.

Let me tell you my truth. I am a life coach, an author, and a motivational speaker. I am a certified aerobics instructor and a personal trainer. I have 20 years' experience in HR Management. I am an entrepreneur and the owner of L.O.V.E. (Life of Victory Enterprises, LLC). I am also the proud mother of one daughter.

I say all this humbly because my life didn't always look this way. Until I published my memoir, *When a Lie Becomes the Truth*, most people didn't know that for many years I went down a path of self-destruction. Because of childhood abuse, lies, and deception, I self-medicated to numb the deep pain and hurt that I felt. I also had several teenage pregnancies.

Currently, I am on a mission to tell my truth to help liberate parents who are suffering the effects of trauma because I know that the truth really does set you free. As a result of the personal development work I've done to overcome the tragedies in my past, I've made amends with myself, I've forgiven myself and everybody else for that matter. Today, I love myself.

Your truth is the path to your purpose. Love yourself enough to tell your truth. Own your truth and set yourself free to experience the fullness of life. You'll find that your story isn't just for you; someone needs your story. The suffering stops when you serve something bigger than yourself. We all have a story. Learn to stand on your powerful story, instead of being stuck in it. When you tell your truth and release it from your spirit, a magical liberating process is set in motion. Are you willing?

Journal Activity #19: Tell your story. What have you done? Where have you been? Who have you loved? Who have you lost? Who have you hurt? Who have you helped? Do you see the value in self-love? Why is self-love important? Validate every aspect of your being. You matter! Every part of your story matters! What do you want the next chapter of your life to look like? What do you want to create now? Write it all out. Tell the truth!

Day 20: Love is an Action Word

**"Love is patient and kind, love is not
envious, or boastful or arrogant or
rude. It does not insist on its own
way, it is not irritable or resentful.
It does not rejoice in wrongdoing,
but rejoices in the truth.
Love never ends."
~ Corinthians 13:4-8**

What does love mean to you?
How do you express love? How do you
share and show love? What makes you
feel loved? The first book of John 4:7-
9 instructs us to "love one another for
love comes from God, and everyone
who loves was born of God and knows
God. Whoever does not love does not
know God because God is love." So,
what is your practical definition of
love?

For me, love is an action word.
Love is as love does. Love is wanting
the best for someone else. Love is
doing your best for yourself and

someone else. I believe that love ought to lift you. I believe love opens your heart, mind, and soul to higher heights, greater joy, and a sense of peace.

We need positive examples of love. As a child my experiences showed me that love hurts. And because of my exposure to dysfunction that is what I reproduced in my adult life. Not until I gave birth to my daughter did I begin to search for a better way. When the student is ready the teacher will appear.

As I searched and met new people from different backgrounds, I realized that love did not have to hurt. I get to choose. I can elevate my thinking. I can design my life, which is exactly what I did. And you can do it too.

I'm not saying that my life changed overnight. It took work and a commitment to a better life. With consistent effort, over time my life improved. Quite honestly, my greatest achievement in life has been breaking the cycle of abuse in my family. When I gave birth to my daughter, I promised myself and God that I would do my best to protect and provide for my child. As a single mother, there were times when I held down three jobs to make ends meet. Love will make you go farther, work harder, and do more than you ever thought possible. The light in my daughter's eyes motivated me to create a better life.

What's your motivation to release the weight? What do you want to change or improve? And why do you want to do it? My daughter was

my "why"? What's your "why"? If you
have a big enough "why," you'll figure
out "how".

Journal Activity #20: If you want
love, be loving. Think about love
today and show love for yourself and
others. In so doing, what did you
discover? What's your definition of
love? How do you express love? How
is your love life? How would you like
your love life to be? How can you
elevate and create more love in your
life?

**"God so loved the world that He
gave His only begotten son that
whosoever believeth in Him should
not perish but have everlasting life."
~ John 3:16**

Day 21: We Get the Life We Create

**"We don't get the life we deserve.
We get the life we create."
~ Anonymous**

Congratulations!

You made it to day 21!

Take time today to assess your progress. What did you want to achieve during this 21 Day Journey and what did you accomplish? Did you write in your journal every day? Did you complete the journal exercises each day? What came up for you? The practice of journaling is therapeutic in and of itself. When you put pen to paper it helps to release your thoughts as well as pinned-up energy. Look back on your journal entries and notice your mind set, notice the thoughts, behaviors, and actions that you wrote about in your journal.

Is there anything you wanted to get done that you put off? There is no judgement here, just notice. Recommit to get it done. Keep your promise to yourself. Let your word mean something. Treat yourself like your best friend. I bet if you promised to do something for your best friend, you would do it. Show up for yourself. Keep your word to yourself. Follow through for yourself. Follow up and be consistent. Find ways to continue to improve. Whether it's reading a book, learning a new skill, travelling to a new destination, or simply taking a walk and enjoying nature, continue your journey of discovery.

It is said that anything you do consistently for 21 days can become habit forming. This is a good start but please keep the momentum going.

To ensure your elevated thinking and action taking, Stay connected to the Facebook Group. Continue to state affirmations daily and continue to write gratitude statements. What you focus on will expand. Repeat this 21-day journey at least three times because if you're like me you need additional support. Reach out to me at CoachJackie@JackieHarden.com. I'd love to support you as you continue your journey to towards freedom.

You have not completely released the weight until you have fully released what has held you back and kept you stuck. When negative self-talk comes up remember to immediately override it with what you know is true: I am capable. I am beautiful, loved, and blessed. I am powerful. I am worthy of financial wealth and abundance. I am enough. I am a child of the Most High God and I deserve every good thing because I am a good person. The more you focus on your positive attributes the more you will empower yourself.

With each new accomplishment, set a new goal. Become masterful at setting and achieving your goals. That's how you make progress; one step and one achievement at a time. Keep the vision of the life you want in mind. Focus on the vision board you created and watch all the things you want come to be. Bring your Mind, Body and Soul into alignment. Find that sweet spot "the zone" where your creative energy flows naturally.

In the zone, you'll experience peace beyond measure. You'll get things done. You'll attract the people, the money, and the energy you desire.

Through prayer and meditation connect with the Ultimate Power of the Universe. Ultimate Power, Infinite Intelligence, the God of your understanding is on your side and will conspire on your behalf. As Les Brown would say: "It's Not Over Until You Win!"

Journal Activity #21: Assess your progress. What did you want to achieve during this 21 Day Journey and what did you accomplish? Did you write in your journal every day? Did you complete the journal exercises each day? Look back on your journal entries and notice your mind set, notice the thoughts, behaviors, and actions that you wrote about in your journal. Where are you now compared to where you began 21 days ago?

Celebrate your successes! Also, please reach out to me via email at CoachJackie@JackieHarden.com and provide feedback regarding your 21-day experience on this journey to create the best version of YOU.

Join the Free Facebook Group:

Best Life Creators
www.facebook.com/groups/2627635074217340/

Visit my website:

www.jackieharden.com to download your free gift, "**Overcoming Limiting Beliefs**."

<u>What If?</u>

What if your dreams really could
come true?
What if it really was up to you?
What if you just had to allow yourself
enough grace,
Enough grace to have a little faith.
What if you took one step forward and
trusted God to take two?
That's all He ever asked of YOU.
What if all your dreams really can
come true?
What if it's all up to YOU?
~ Jackie Harden

About the Author

Jackie Harden is a strategic life and relationship coach, a best-selling author, and a motivational speaker, who resides in the Atlanta, Georgia area.

Over the past 30+ years, she has transformed her life from a struggling single mother to a six-figure professional and entrepreneur. For decades, Jackie Harden was viewed as a hard-working single mother. She spent years working three jobs to make ends meet, all while being enrolled in school and leading different parent organizations.

But what people didn't realize behind her smile was her internal battle, which has become an incredible testimony. That testimony led Jackie to write her first book,

When a Lie Becomes the Truth, a personal memoir about uncovering deeply held family secrets that involve abuse, lies, and deception. In the process of discovering her true identity, Jackie struggled with the guilt and shame associated with abuse, drug addiction, and other forms of self-inflicted pain.

The book chronicles Jackie's journey of self-discovery — from pain to creating a life of prosperity.

Since releasing the book, Jackie has dedicated herself to empowering others by helping them discover their own truth to move forward beyond the pain of the past to create the life of their dreams.

Jackie is passionate about creating opportunities to speak with women and girls all over the nation and working with them to transform their circumstances so they can lead lives of integrity, authenticity, and unconditional love, thereby, positively impacting families, communities, and the world.

Visit www.jackieharden.com to download your free gift, "**Overcoming Limiting Beliefs**" and to learn more about Jackie's programs and offerings. You can also connect with her on social media:

- https://www.facebook.com/jaciehardenlifecoach
- https://www.instagram.com/jackievharden
- https://www.linkedin.com/in/jackievharden

Facebook Group "Best Life Creators"
www.facebook.com/groups/2627635074217340/

Made in the USA
Middletown, DE
12 December 2023